AF496536

# Blues

## 23 classic songs for keyboard




Published 1995

**Series Editor** Anna Joyce
**Design & Art Direction** Dominic Brookman

Music arranged & processed by Barnes Music Engraving Ltd East Sussex TN34 1HA
Cover Image Count Basie © Michael Ochs Archive/Redferns Music Picture Library

© International Music Publications Ltd
Griffin House 161 Hammersmith Road London England W6 8BS

# All Your Love

Words and Music by Otis Rush

**Suggested Registration:** Jazz Organ
**Rhythm:** Rhythm & Blues
**Tempo:** ♩ = 112

Fm
I have in store for you.____ Well, I love you
C7          B♭m          Fm
ba - by,____ I know you love me too.____
F
Oh, oh, oh ba - by,____ you know I
B♭
love you,____ yeah, yeah, yeah ba - by,____
F
you know I love you ba - by,____ I love
C7          B♭          F
__ you ba - by,____ oh, I love you so.________
B♭     B♭m     C7     F     Fm

# Basin St Blues

Words and Music by Spencer Williams

**Suggested Registration:** Clarinet
**Rhythm:** Swing
**Tempo:** ♩ = 92

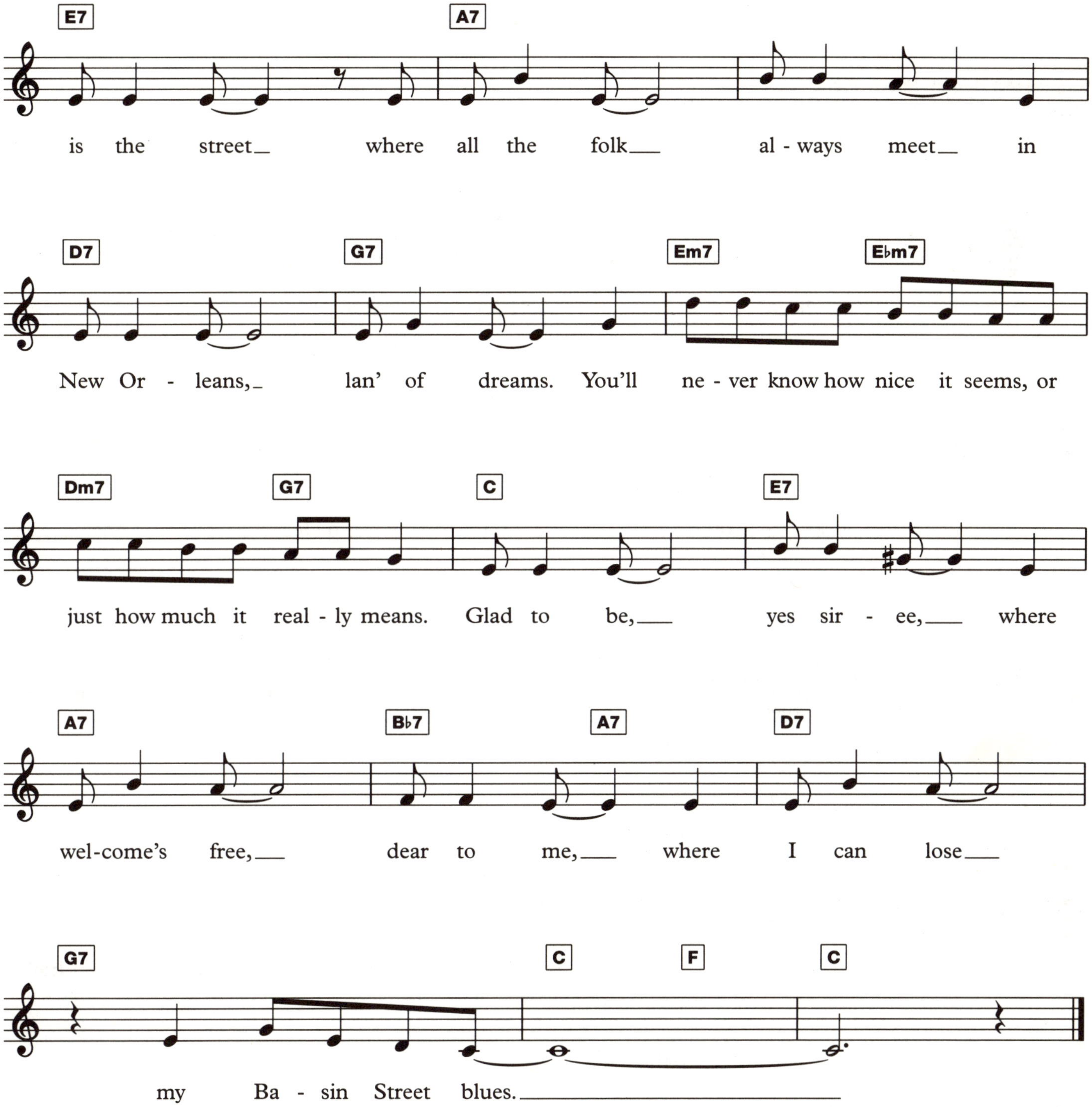

E7 A7
is the street_ where all the folk_ al - ways meet_ in
D7 G7 Em7 E♭m7
New Or - leans,_ lan' of dreams. You'll ne - ver know how nice it seems, or
Dm7 G7 C E7
just how much it real - ly means. Glad to be,_ yes sir - ee,_ where
A7 B♭7 A7 D7
wel-come's free,_ dear to me,_ where I can lose_
G7 C F C
my Ba - sin Street blues._

A7
B♭7
C
D7
Dm7
E♭m7
E7
Em7
F
G7

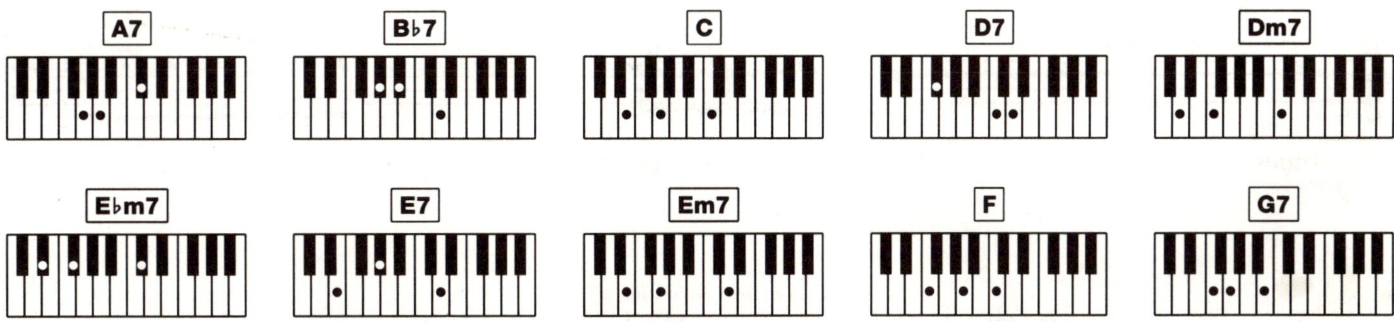

# The Birth Of The Blues

Words by B G De Sylva and Lew Brown / Music by Ray Henderson

**Suggested Registration:** Piano
**Rhythm:** Slow Swing
**Tempo:** ♩ = 100

E7    Bm7♭5    E7    Bm7♭5    E7
_ they took a new___ note,_______ pushed it through a
A7    D7
horn till it was worn___ in - to a blue___ note,
G7    C    G7
and then they nursed it, re - hearsed__ it, and gave
C    E7    F    D7    G7
_ out the news_____ that the South___ land_____
C    F    C
_ gave birth___ to the blues._____________
A7    Bm7♭5    C    D7    E7
F    G7

# BLACK MAGIC WOMAN

*Words and Music by Peter A Green*

**Suggested Registration:** Electric Guitar
**Rhythm:** Mambo / Latin Rock
**Tempo:** ♩ = 112

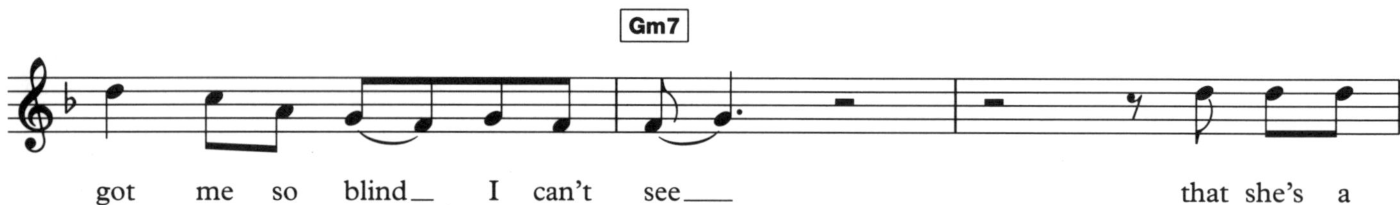

Gm7
Stop mess-ing round_ with your tricks._ Don't turn your
Dm7   Am7   Dm7
back on me ba-by, you just might pick up my__ ma-gic sticks.
You got your spell on me ba - by, got your spell on me ba-
Am7   Dm7
- by, yes, you got your spell on me ba-by,
Gm7
turn-in' my heart_ in-to stone._ I
Dm7   Am7   Dm7
need you so bad ma-gic wo-man, I can't leave you a - lone.________

Am7   Dm7   Gm7

# Blue And Sentimental

Words and Music by Count Basie, Jerry Livingston, Charles Hathaway and Mack David

**Suggested Registration:** Vibraphone
**Rhythm:** Slow Swing
**Tempo:** ♩ = 80

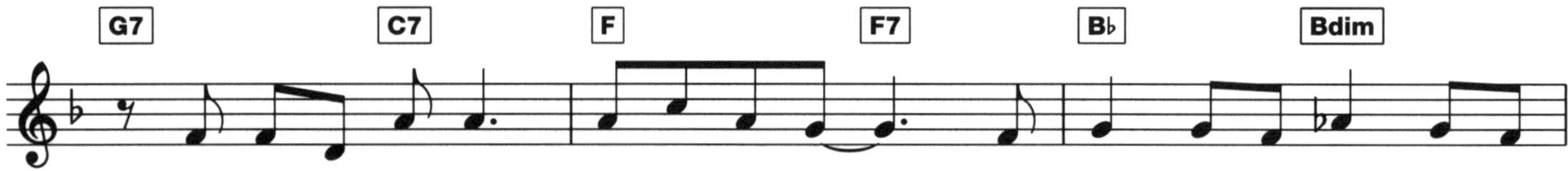

just won't-come-true dreams, I find. Blue and sen - ti - men - tal,
I can't for - get you, my heart won't let you out of my mind. It
rains all the time since you said good - bye,__ the skies and my eyes, and my
heart all cry.__ Blue and sen - ti - men - tal, if you don't want me,
why do you haunt me, and keep me feel - ing blue and sen - ti - men-tal?____

# Brother, Can You Spare A Dime?

Words by E Y Harburg / Music by Jay Gorney

**Suggested Registration:** Vibraphone
**Rhythm:** Swing
**Tempo:** ♩ = 92

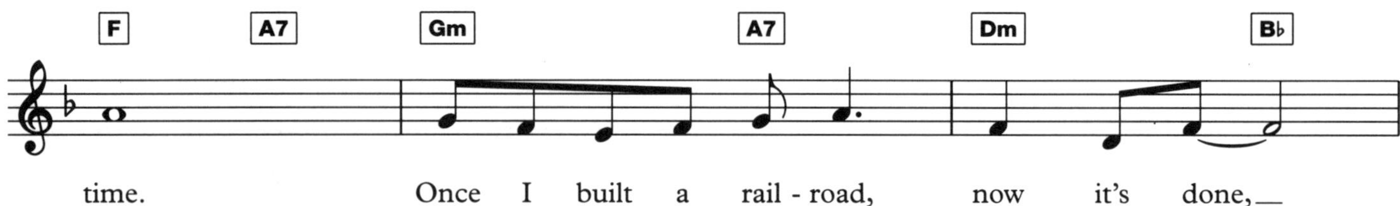


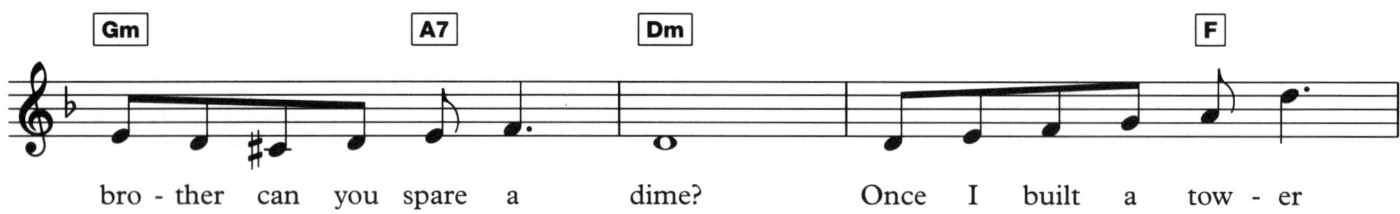

dime? Once in kha - ki suits, gee, we looked swell,
full of that Yan - kee Doo-dle - de - dum. Half a mil - lion boots went
slog - gin' though hell, and I was the kid___ with the drum.___
Say, don't you re-mem-ber, they called me 'Al?'_ It was 'Al' all the time.
Say, don't you re-mem-ber, I'm your pal?_ Bud-dy can you spare a dime?
A7  B♭  C7  D7  Dm
E7  F  G  Gm

# Cocaine

Words and Music by J J Cale

**Suggested Registration:** Electric Guitar
**Rhythm:** Latin Rock / 8 Beat
**Tempo:** ♩ = 108

got bad news_ you want to kick them blues, Co - caine._
When your day is done,_ and you wan - na run,_ Co - caine.
_ She don't lie,____ she don't lie,__ she don't lie,_
_ Co - caine.__ She don't lie,_
_ she don't lie,__ she don't lie,___ Co - caine._
B7 C D E E7
Em G

# CROSSROADS

Words and Music by Robert L Johnson

**Suggested Registration:** Saxophone
**Rhythm:** Rhythm & Blues / Rock
**Tempo:** ♩ = 120

© 1975, 1978 & 1995 Getaway Music Ltd, Rightsong Music Inc and Gunnell Music Inc, USA
Warner Chappell Music Ltd, London W1Y 3FA

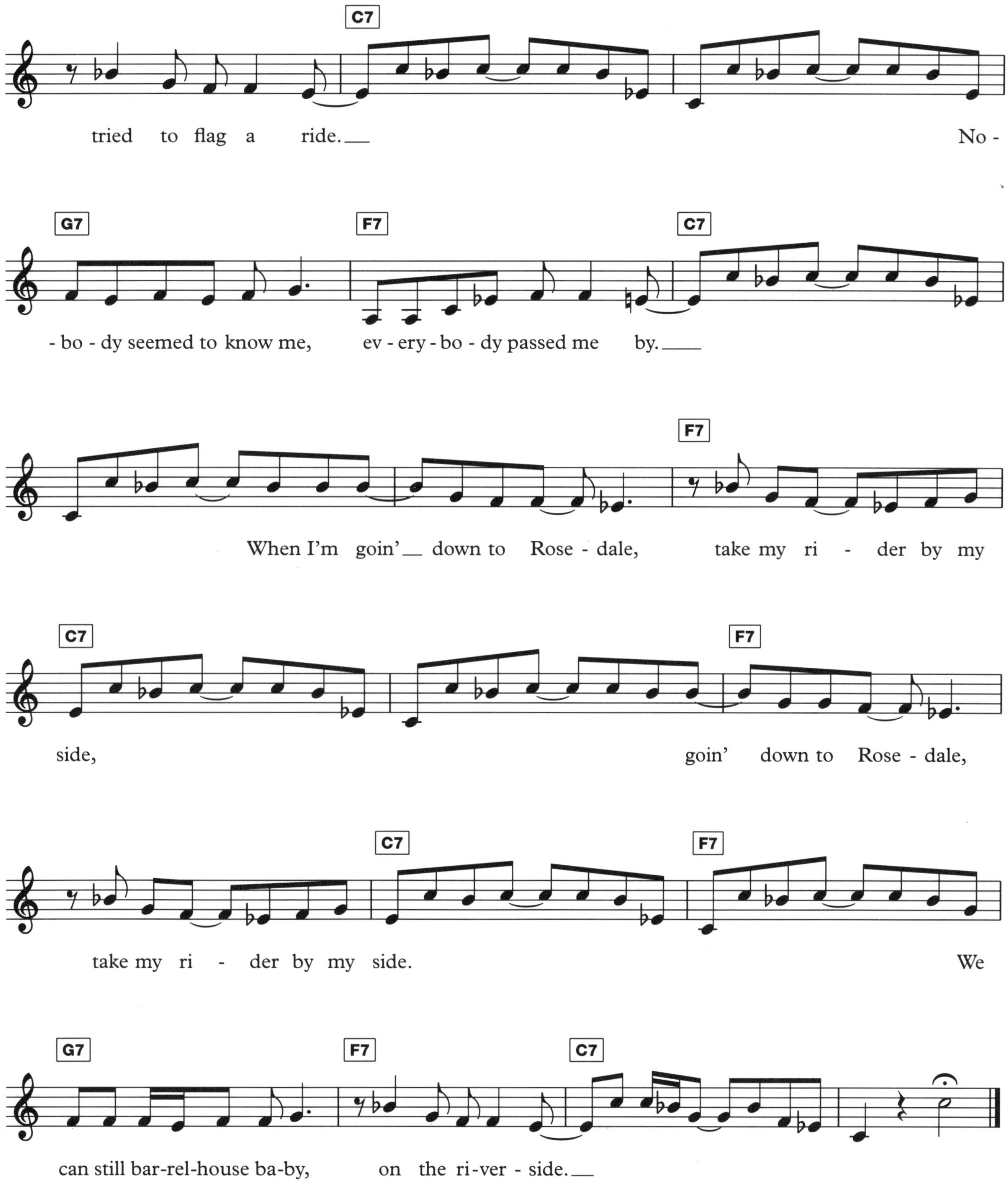

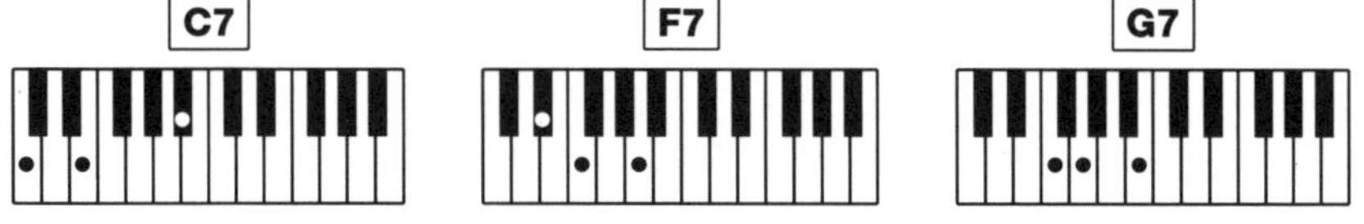
C7
tried to flag a ride.__ No -

G7      F7      C7
- bo - dy seemed to know me, ev - ery - bo - dy passed me by.__

F7
When I'm goin'__ down to Rose - dale, take my ri - der by my

C7      F7
side, goin' down to Rose - dale,

C7      F7
take my ri - der by my side. We

G7      F7      C7
can still bar-rel-house ba-by, on the ri-ver-side.__

C7      F7      G7

# Don't Dream Of Anybody But Me
## (Li'l Darlin')

By Neal Hefti

**Suggested Registration:** Muted Trumpet
**Rhythm:** Slow Swing
**Tempo:** ♩ = 76

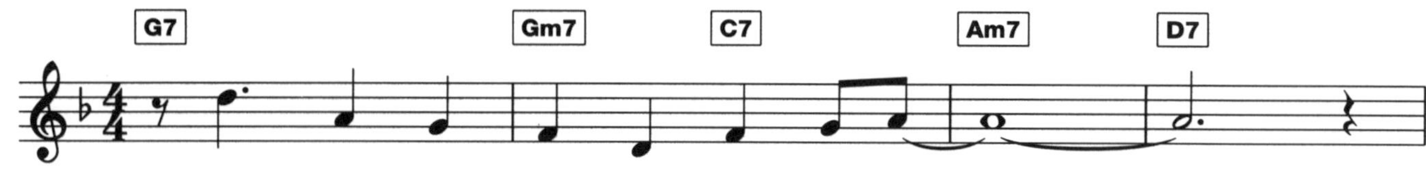


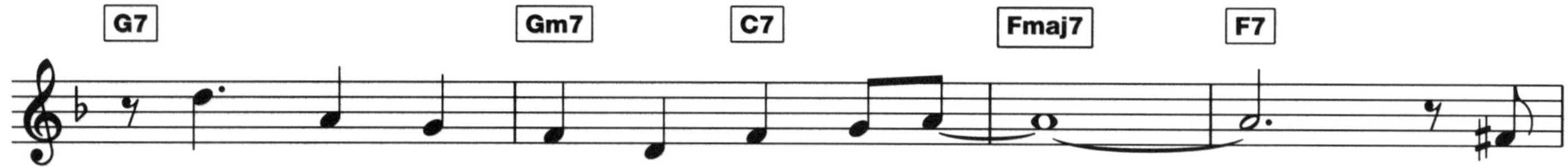

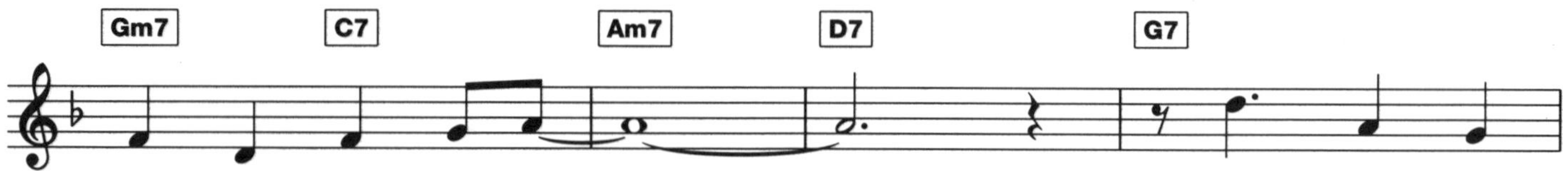

# FRANKIE AND JOHNNY

Traditional

**Suggested Registration:** Clarinet
**Rhythm:** Swing
**Tempo:** ♩ = 108

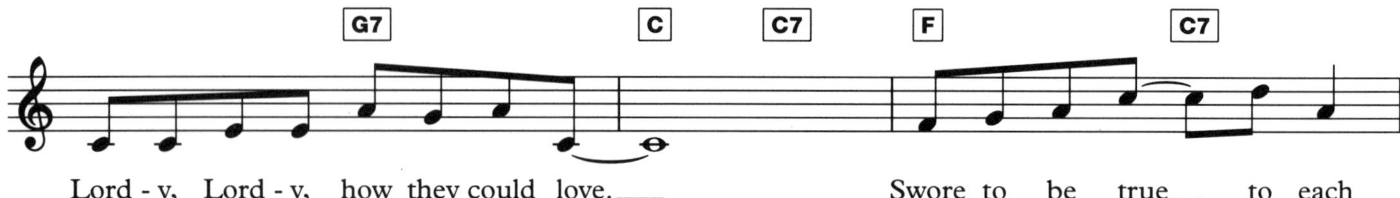

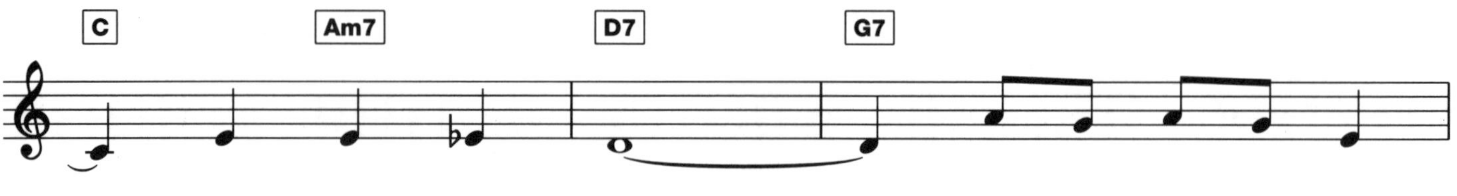

C  F  G7  C  G7
John - ny said, 'I've got to
C  G7  C  C7
leave you, but I won't be very long.
F  C7  F  F#dim
Don't you wait up for me hon - ey, or wor - ry while I'm gone.
C  Am7  D7  G7
I am your man, I would - n't do you
C  F  C  Am7  D7
wrong.'
G7  C  F  C
Am7  C  C7  D7  F
F#dim  G7

# Georgia On My Mind

Words by Stuart Gorrell / Music by Hoagy Carmichael

**Suggested Registration:** Jazz Organ
**Rhythm:** Slow Rock
**Tempo:** ♩ = 72

Dm        Gm7        Dm        G7        Dm        A7
oth - er   eyes___   smile   ten - der - ly,___   still   in   peace - ful


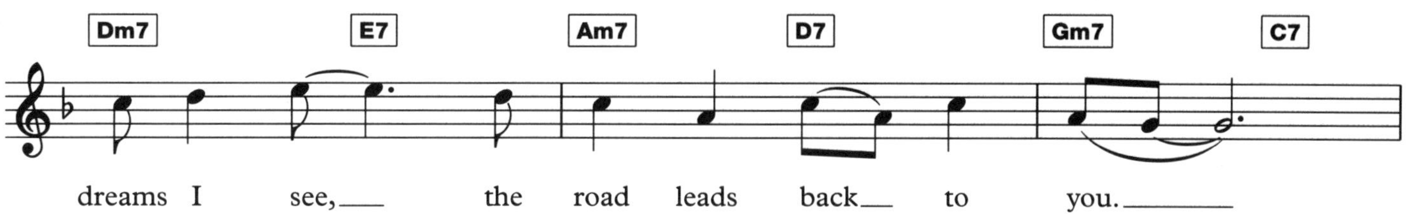

Dm7        E7        Am7        D7        Gm7        C7
dreams   I   see,___   the   road   leads   back___   to   you.___


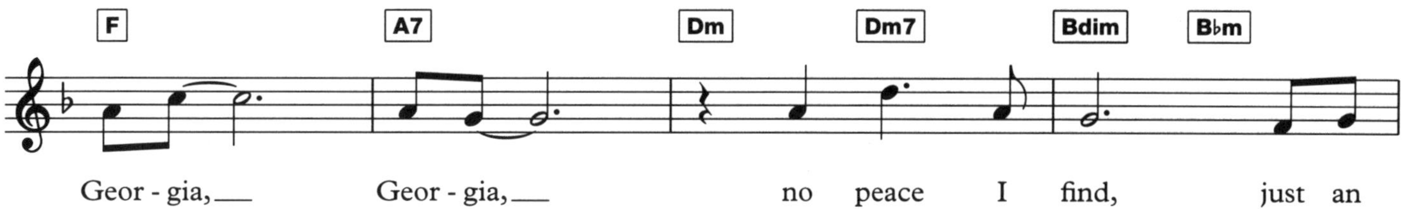

F        A7        Dm        Dm7        Bdim        Bbm
Geor - gia,___   Geor - gia,___   no   peace   I   find,   just   an


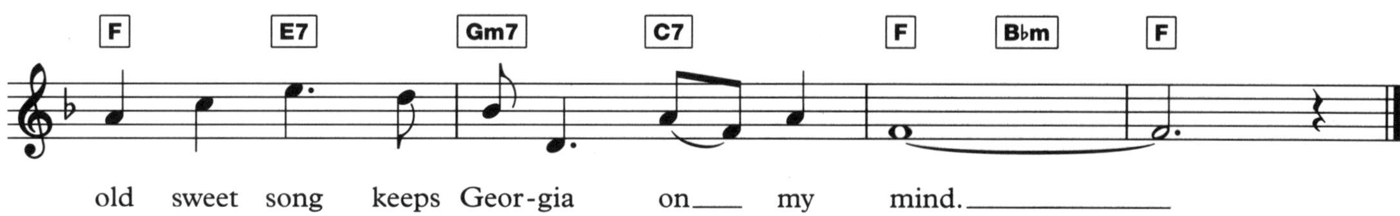

F        E7        Gm7        C7        F        Bbm        F
old   sweet   song   keeps   Geor-gia   on___   my   mind.___


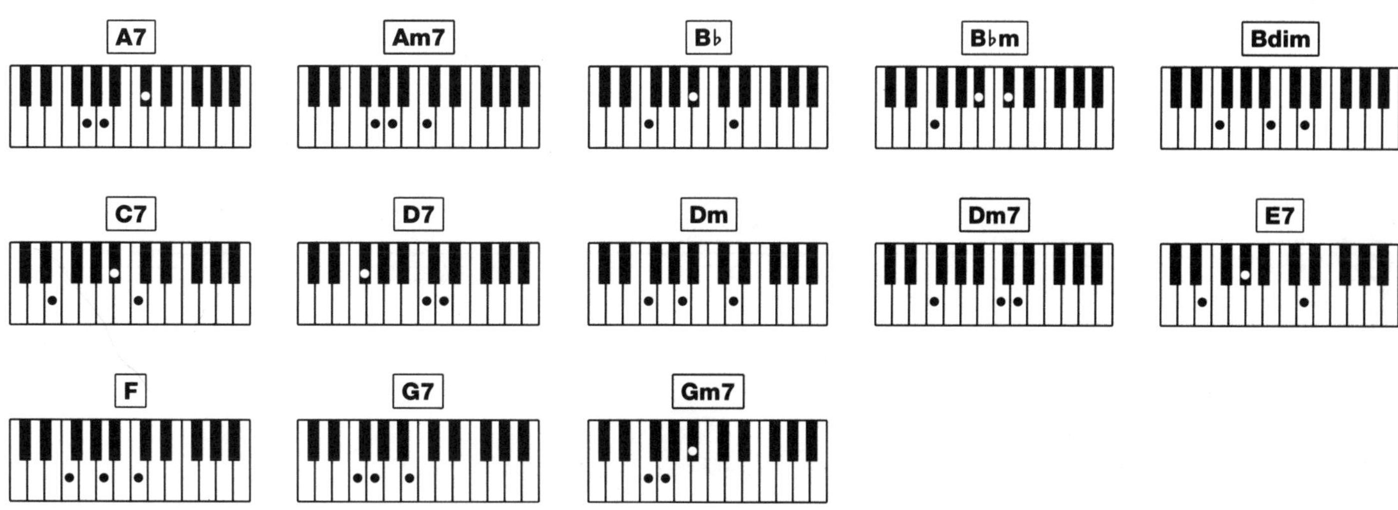

A7        Am7        Bb        Bbm        Bdim
C7        D7        Dm        Dm7        E7
F        G7        Gm7

# God Bless The Child

Words and Music by Arthur Herzog Jr and Billie Holiday

**Suggested Registration:** Electric Piano
**Rhythm:** Slow Rock 6/8
**Tempo:** ♩. = 60

© 1941 & 1995 Edward B Marks Music Co, USA
Carlin Music Corp, London NW1 8BD

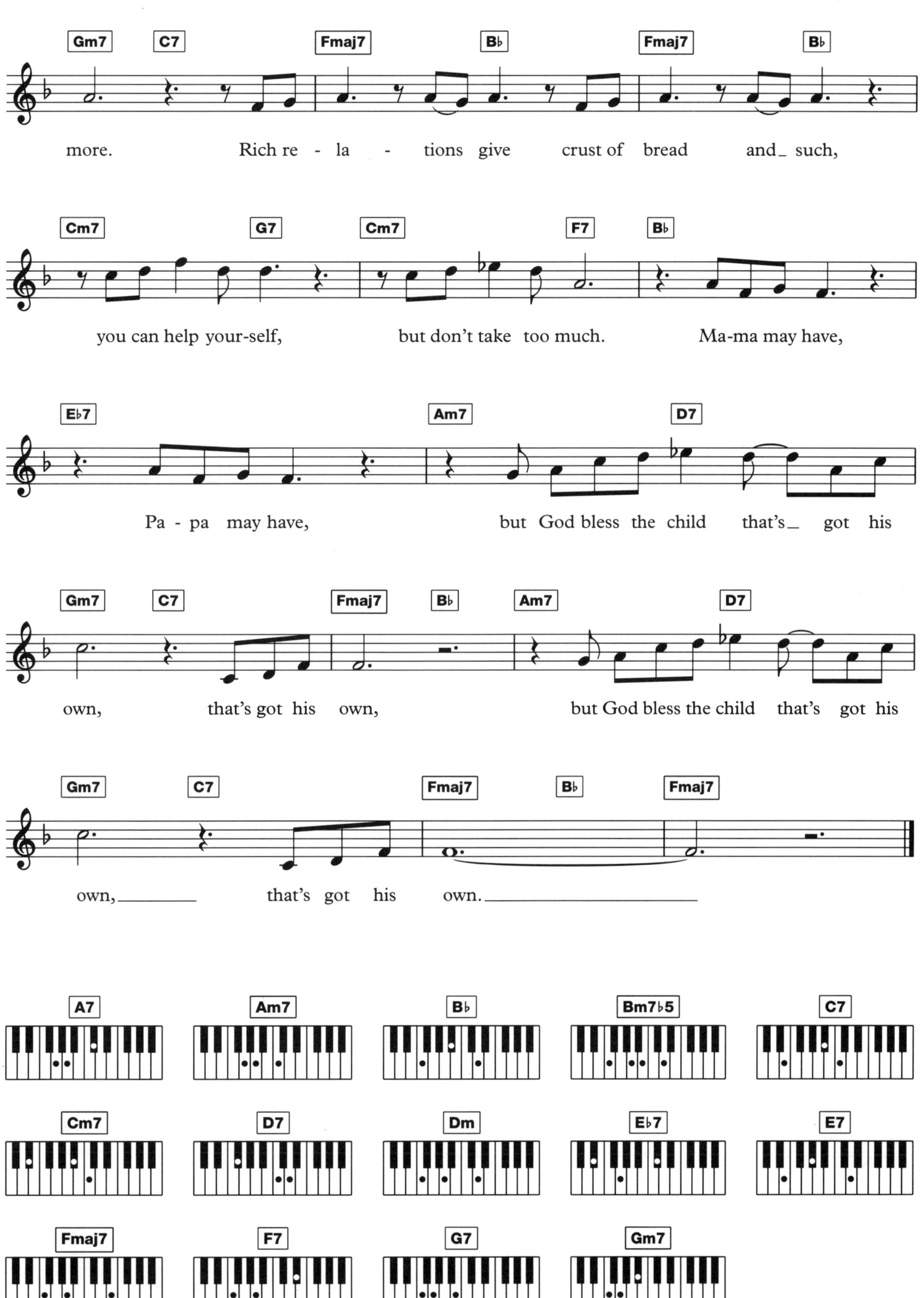
Gm7   C7   Fmaj7   B♭   Fmaj7   B♭
more.   Rich re - la - tions give   crust of   bread   and_ such,
Cm7   G7   Cm7   F7   B♭
you can help your-self,   but don't take too much.   Ma-ma may have,
E♭7   Am7   D7
Pa - pa   may have,   but God bless the child   that's_   got his
Gm7   C7   Fmaj7   B♭   Am7   D7
own,   that's got his   own,   but God bless the child   that's   got his
Gm7   C7   Fmaj7   B♭   Fmaj7
own,_______   that's got his   own._______
A7   Am7   B♭   Bm7♭5   C7
Cm7   D7   Dm   E♭7   E7
Fmaj7   F7   G7   Gm7

# Good-Bye Blues

Words and Music by Dorothy Fields, Jimmy McHugh and Arnold Johnson

**Suggested Registration:** Vibraphone
**Rhythm:** Swing
**Tempo:** ♩ = 192

D7        G7
Lost     two     lov - in'     arms

C7
I        used        to        use

F        Cdim        C7
lone  -  some        nights.

E7        A7
Low        down        news,        now        she        might

D7        Gm7
be        I        don't        know        whose,        I've        got        those

G7        C7        F
Good        Good  -  bye        Blues,

A7        Bb        C7        Cdim        D7
E7        Eaug5        F        G7        Gm7

# I Ain't Got Nothing But The Blues

Words by Don George / Music by Duke Ellington

**Suggested Registration:** Harmonica
**Rhythm:** Slow Swing
**Tempo:** ♩ = 84

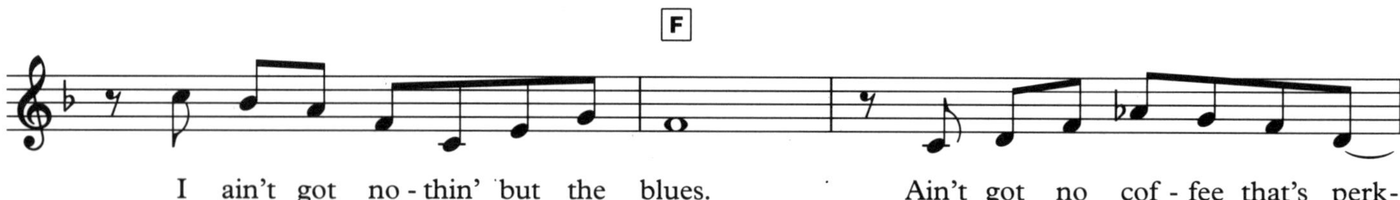

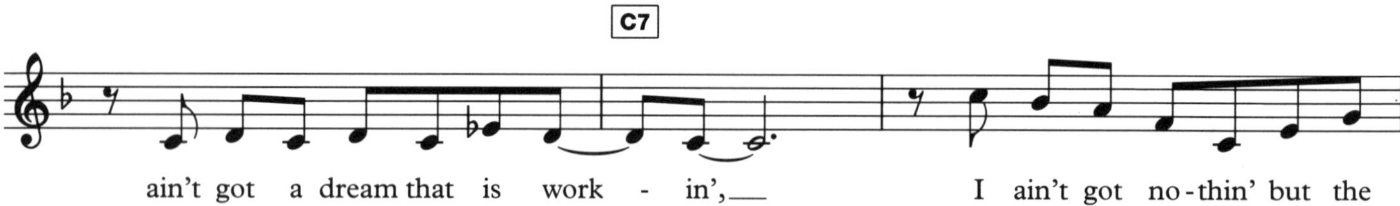

D7
hair up,___ I just can't make it come down.___ Be - lieve me,
G7
Pap - py,___ I can't get hap - py,___ since my ev - er - lov - in' ba - by left town.
C7
F
___ Ain't got no rest on my slum - ber, ain't got no feel-ings to bruise,
Bb
C7
___ ain't got no te - le - phone num - ber,___
F Bb F
I ain't got no - thin' but the blues._______
A7 Bb C7 D7 F
G7

# Little Red Rooster

Words and Music by Willie Dixon

**Suggested Registration:** Harmonica
**Rhythm:** Slow Rock
**Tempo:** ♩ = 76

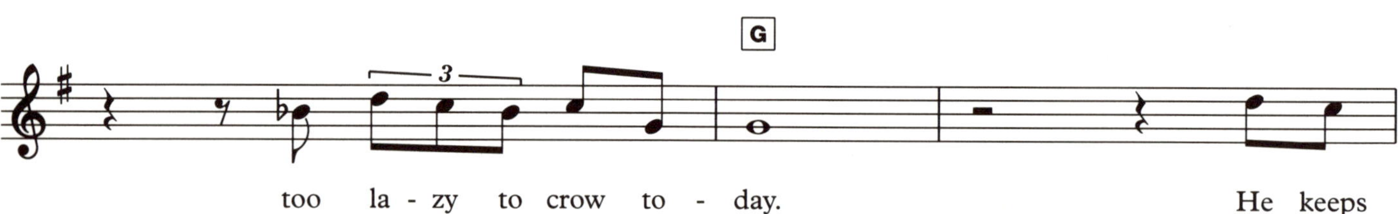


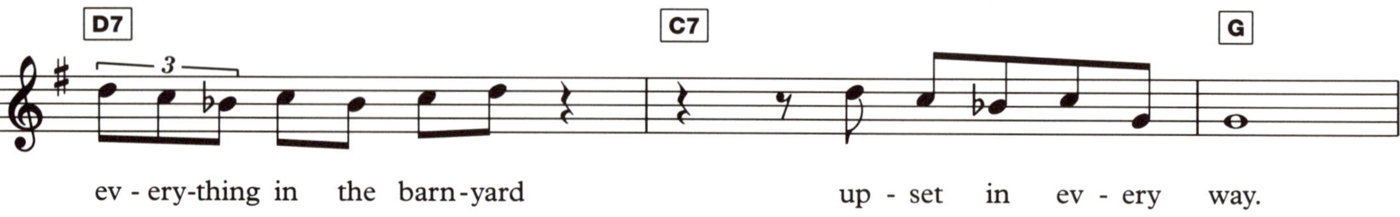

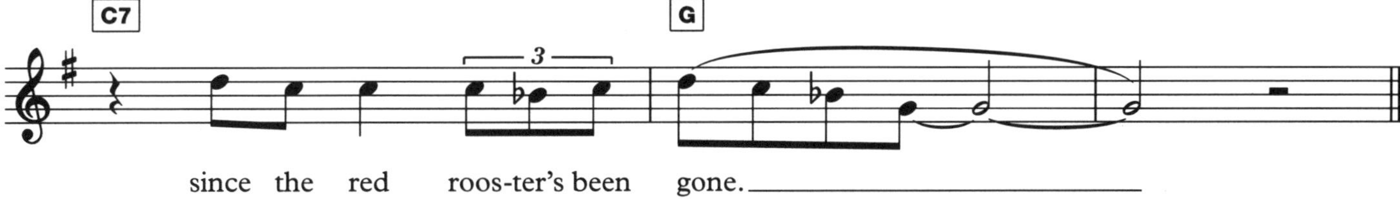
G
the hound be - gin to howl.
Watch
D7
C7
3
G
out all you hen-folk,
my lit - tle red roos-ter's on the prowl.
D7
G
C7
Now if you see my red roos - ter,
send him
G
C7
home.
I said, if you see my red roos - ter,
G
D7
3
send him home.
I've had no peace in the barn-yard
C7
3
G
since the red roos-ter's been gone.

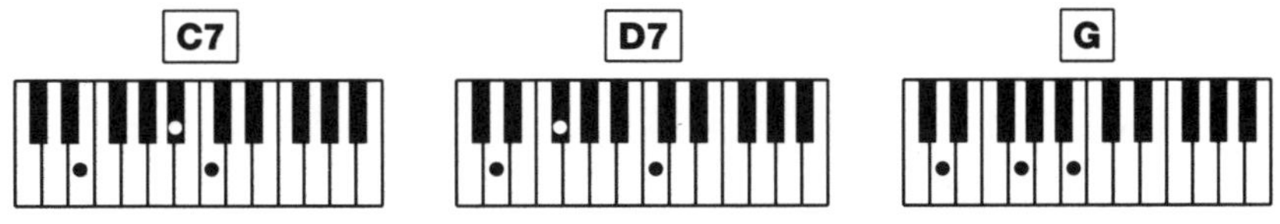
C7
D7
G

# Mood Indigo

Words and Music by Duke Ellington, Irving Mills and Albany Bigard

**Suggested Registration:** Vibraphone
**Rhythm:** Slow Swing
**Tempo:** ♩ = 84

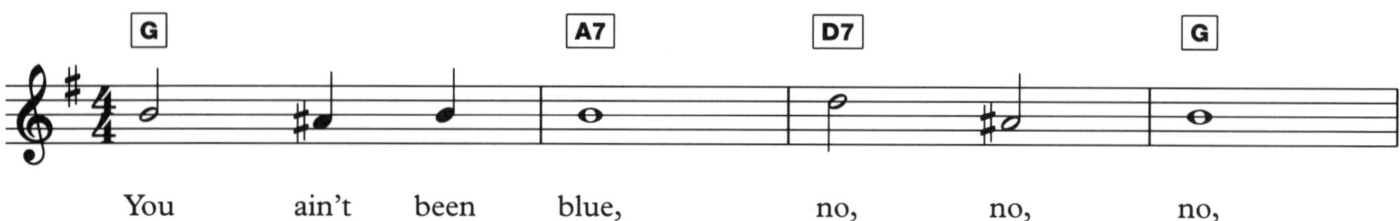


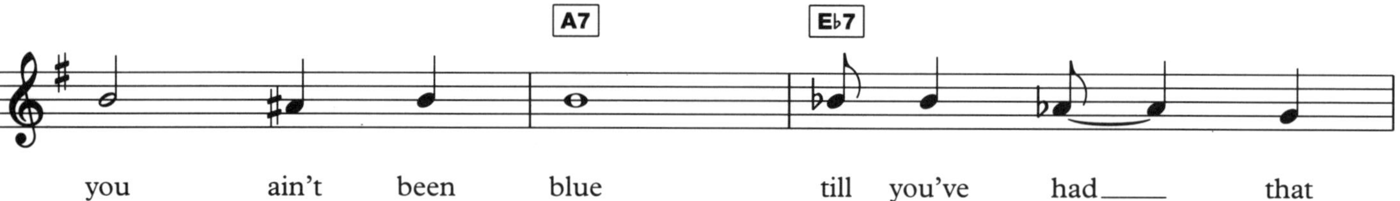

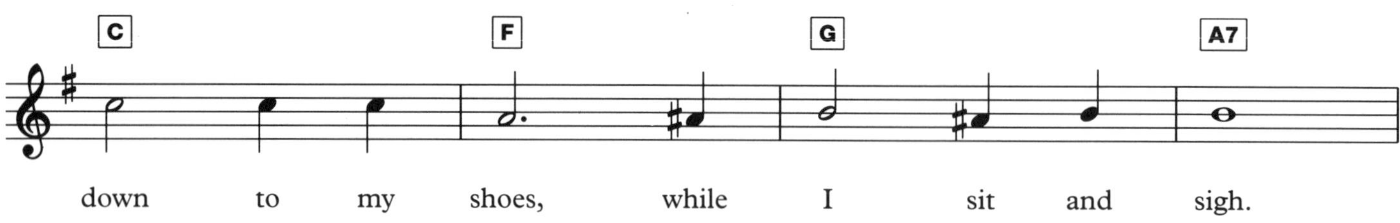


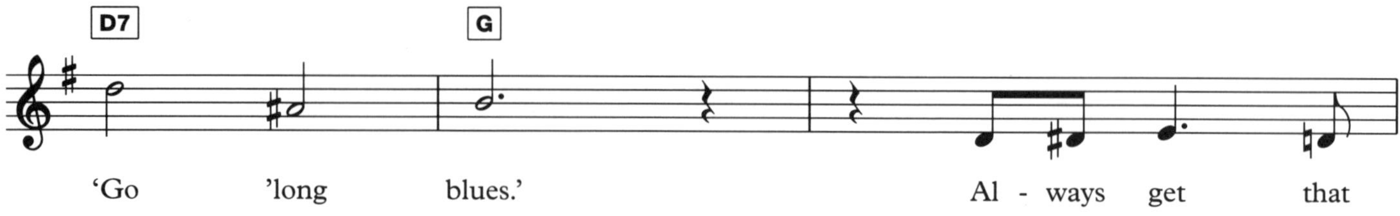

A7
D7
G
mood in - di - go,___ since my ba - by said good bye.

A7
In the eve - nin' when lights are low,__ I'm so lone-some I could

D7
G7
cry, 'cause there's no - bo - dy who cares a - bout me.__

C7
G
I'm just a soul who's blu - er than blue__ can be. When I get that

A7
D7
G
mood in - di - go,___ I could lay me down and die.

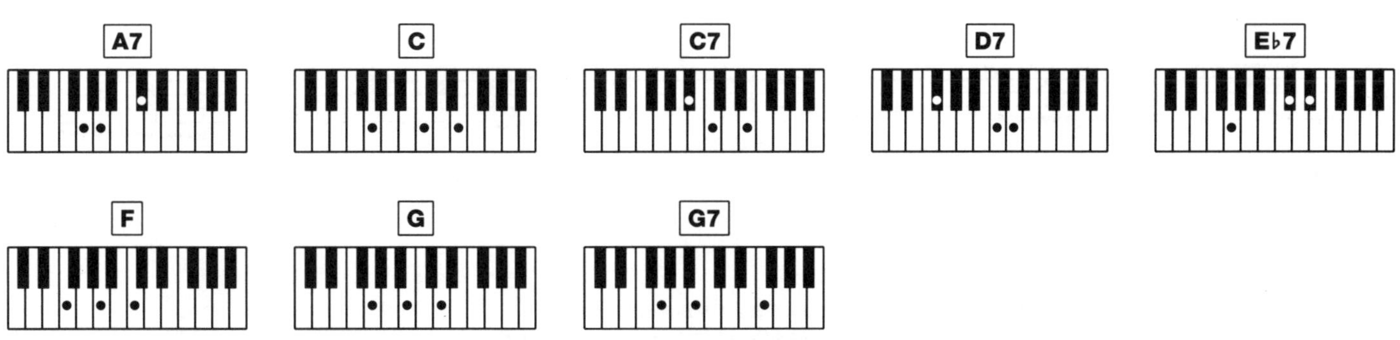
A7
C
C7
D7
E♭7
F
G
G7

# Mustang Sally

Words and Music by Bonny Rice

**Suggested Registration:** Jazz Organ
**Rhythm:** Rhythm & Blues
**Tempo:** ♩ = 120

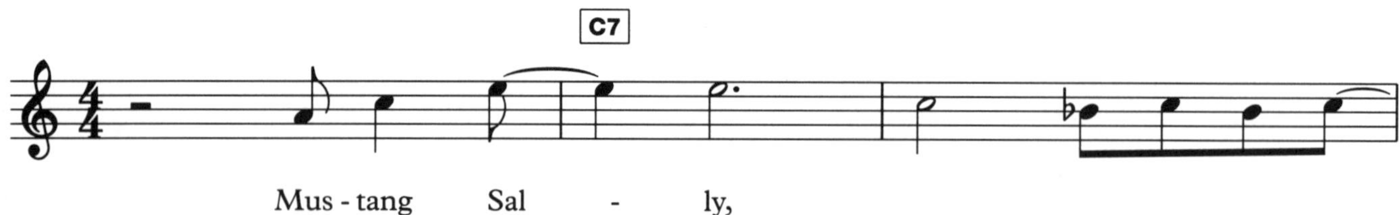

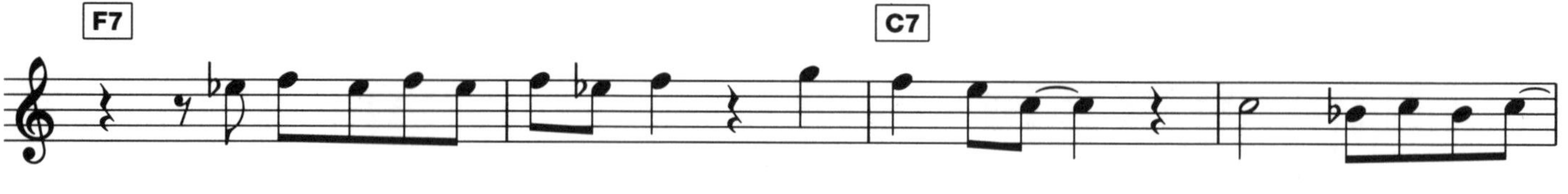

All you wan-na do is ride__ a-round Sal-ly,
(ride Sal - ly____ ride,) __ all you wan-na do is ride__ a-round Sal - ly,
F7
(ride Sal - ly____ ride,) __ all you wan-na do is ride__ a-round Sal -ly,
C7
(ride Sal - ly____ ride,) __ all you wan-na do is ride__ a-round Sal - ly,
G7
(ride Sal - ly____ ride.) __ One of these ear - ly morn - ings,
F7
C7
I'm gon - na be wip - in' those_ weep - in' eyes.________

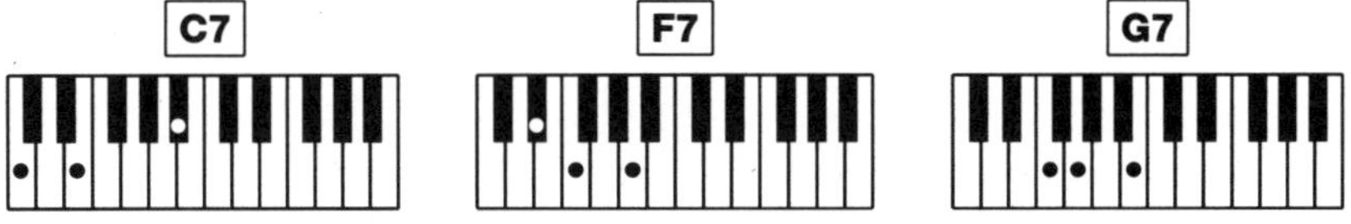
C7
F7
G7

# St Louis Blues

Words and Music by W C Handy

**Suggested Registration:** Muted trumpet
**Rhythm:** Swing
**Tempo:** ♩ = 108

© 1914 & 1995 Handy Brothers Music Co Inc, USA
Francis Day & Hunter Ltd, London WC2H 0EA

G
D7
I'll pack my trunk,
G
make ma get - a - way. Got de
St. Lou - is Blues, jes' as blue as ah can be.
G7
C
Dat man got a heart lak a rock cast in the sea,
G
D7
or else he would - n't have gone
G
so far from me.
C
D7
G
G7

# STILL GOT THE BLUES

*Words and Music by Gary Moore*

**Suggested Registration:** Distorted Guitar
**Rhythm:** Slow Rock 6/8
**Tempo:** ♩. = 52

G7
Cmaj7
Fmaj7
that love________ was no friend of mine,__
Bm7♭5
E7
but I should have known time________ af -
Am
Em
- ter time.________ So________ long,________ it was
Am
D7
F7
so________ long a - go,________ but I've still________ got the
E7
Am
blues________ for you.________________
Am
Bm7♭5
Cmaj7
D7
Dm7
E7
Em
Fmaj7
F7
G7

# Swing Low Sweet Chariot

Traditional

**Suggested Registration:** Harmonica
**Rhythm:** Soft Rock
**Tempo:** ♩ = 88

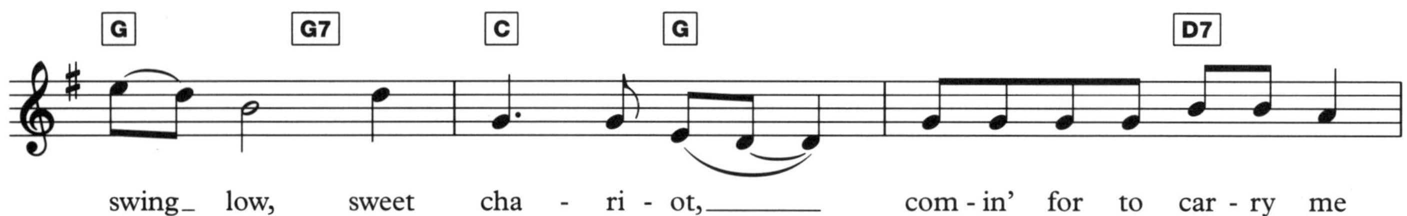

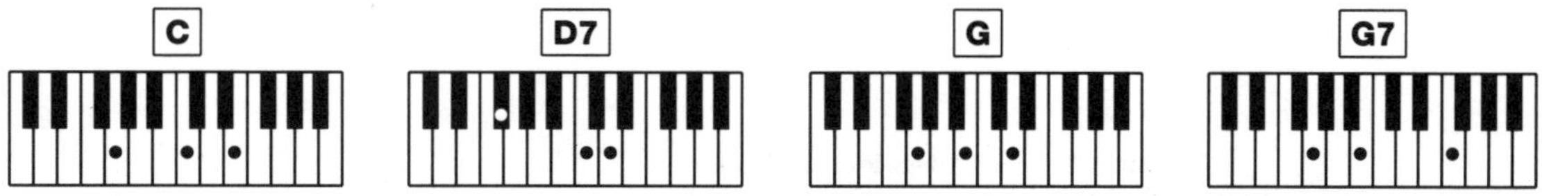

C        G
look o - ver Jor - dan, and what do I see________

D7        G    G7
com - in' for to car - ry me home? A band__ of an - gels

C        G        D7
com - in' af - ter me,_________ com - in' for to car - ry me

G        C    G
home. Swing low, sweet cha - ri - ot,_________

D7        G    G7
com - in' for to car - ry me home, swing__ low, sweet

C    G        D7    G
cha - ri - ot,________ com - in' for to car - ry me home.

C    D7    G    G7

# Swingin' Shepherd Blues

Words by Rhoda Roberts and Ken Jacobson / Music by Moe Koffman

**Suggested Registration:** Saxophone
**Rhythm:** Shuffle
**Tempo:** ♩ = 126

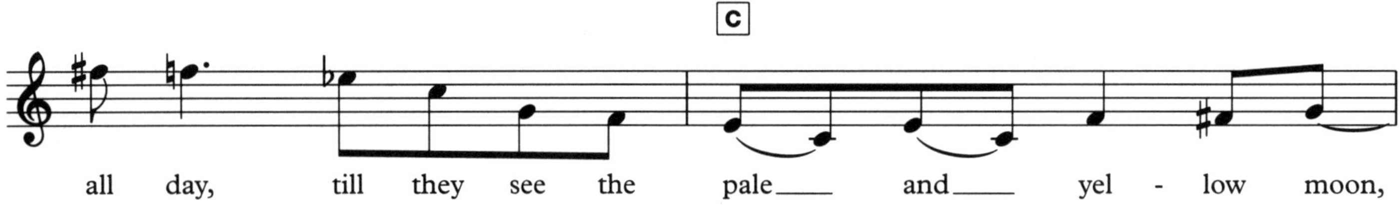


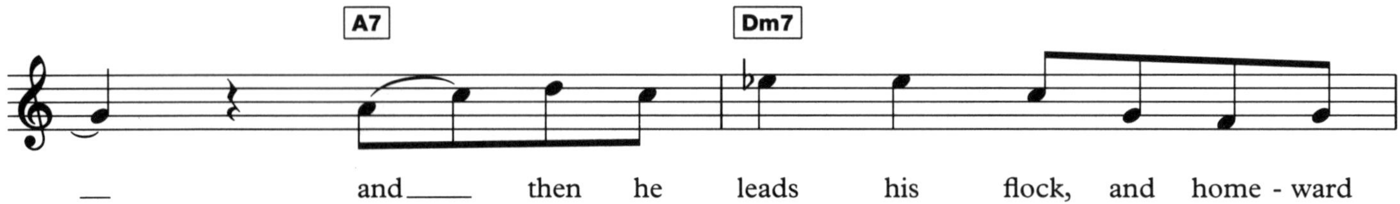

F
C
Come home shep - herd, let it e - cho
A7
Dm7
G7
through the hills,___ the swing - in' shep - herd___
C
G7
C
blues. Come home
C7
F
shep herd, play those haunt - ing trills. Come home
C
A7
shep - herd, let it e - cho through the hills,___ the
Dm7
G7
C
swing - in' shep - herd___ blues.___________
A7
C
C7
Dm7
F
G7

# Watermelon Man

By Herbie Hancock

**Suggested Registration:** Jazz Organ
**Rhythm:** Rhythm & Blues
**Tempo:** ♩ = 112

Oh! Wa - ter - me - lon Man.

F7
C7
Ah! Wa - ter - me - lon Man.

G7
F7
They are just as round as they can be,

G7
F7
G7
make you al - most want to eat the seeds, Ev - ery - bo - dy dig


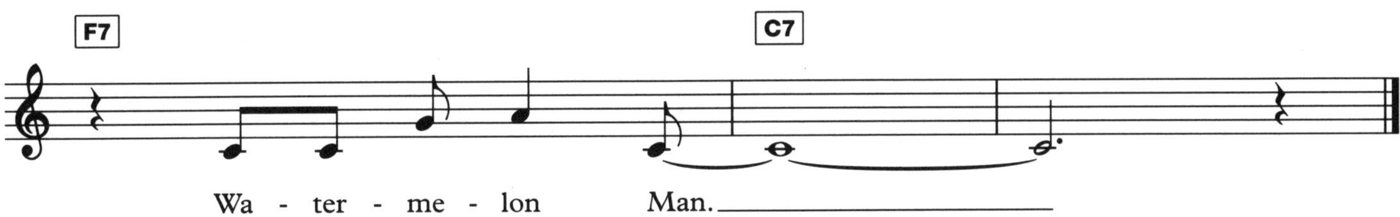

F7
C7
Wa - ter - me - lon Man.


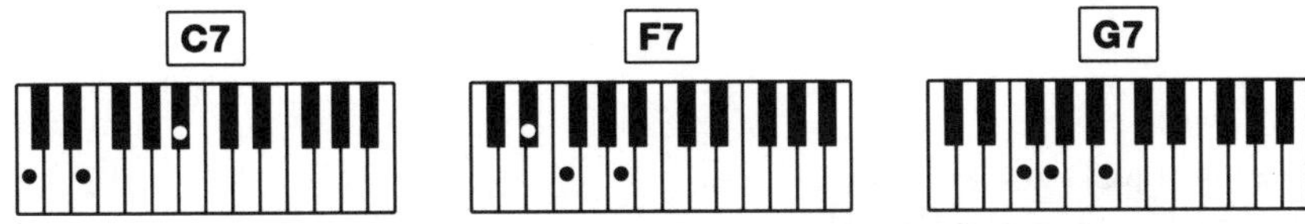

C7
F7
G7

# Work Song

By Nat Adderly

**Suggested Registration:** Saxophone
**Rhythm:** Swing
**Tempo:** ♩ = 152

D7
Gm
G7
C7
D7
Gm
G7
C7
D7
Gm
C7
D7
G7
Gm

# THE EASY KEYBOARD LIBRARY

## Also available in the Decades Series

### THE TWENTIES
#### including:

Ain't Misbehavin'  
Ain't She Sweet?  
Baby Face  
The Man I Love

My Blue Heaven  
Side By Side  
Spread A Little Happiness  
When You're Smiling

---

### THE THIRTIES
#### including:

All Of Me  
A Fine Romance  
I Wanna Be Loved By You  
I've Got You Under My Skin

The Lady Is A Tramp  
Smoke Gets In Your Eyes  
Summertime  
Walkin' My Baby Back Home

---

### THE FORTIES
#### including:

Almost Like Being In Love  
Don't Get Around Much Any More  
How High The Moon  
Let There Be Love

Sentimental Journey  
Swinging On A Star  
Tenderly  
You Make Me Feel So Young

---

### THE FIFTIES
#### including:

All The Way  
Cry Me A River  
Dream Lover  
High Hopes

Magic Moments  
Mister Sandman  
A Teenager In Love  
Whatever Will Be Will Be

---

### THE SIXTIES
#### including:

Cabaret  
Happy Birthday Sweet Sixteen  
I'm A Believer  
The Loco-motion

My Kind Of Girl  
Needles And Pins  
There's A Kind Of Hush  
Walk On By

---

### THE SEVENTIES
#### including:

Chanson D'Amour  
Hi Ho Silver Lining  
I'm Not In Love  
Isn't She Lovely

Save Your Kisses For Me  
Take Good Care Of My Baby  
We've Only Just Begun  
You Light Up My Life

---

### THE EIGHTIES
#### including:

Anything For You  
China In Your Hand  
Everytime You Go Away  
Golden Brown

I Want To Break Free  
Karma Chameleon  
Nikita  
Take My Breath Away

---

### THE NINETIES
#### including:

Crocodile Shoes  
I Swear  
A Million Love Songs  
The One And Only

Promise Me  
Sacrifice  
Think Twice  
Would I Lie To You?

## THE EASY KEYBOARD LIBRARY